Lerner SPORTS

SPORTS ALL-ST★RS

KYRIE IRVING

Martha London

Lerner Publications ◆ Minneapolis

Lerner Publications Company
A division of Lerner Publishing Group, Inc.
241 First Avenue North
Minneapolis, MN 55401 USA

For reading levels and more information, look up this title at www.lernerbooks.com.

Main body text set in Albany Std.
Typeface provided by Agfa.

Library of Congress Cataloging-in-Publication Data
Names: London, Martha, author.
Title: Kyrie Irving / by Martha London.
Description: Minneapolis : Lerner Publications, [2020] | Series: Sports All-Stars | Includes bibliographical references and index.
Identifiers: LCCN 2018060925 (print) | LCCN 2019008211 (ebook) | ISBN 9781541556140 (library binding : alk. paper) | ISBN 9781541574502 (paperback : alk. paper) | ISBN 9781541556249 (eb pdf)
Subjects: LCSH: Irving, Kyrie, 1992-–Juvenile literature. | Basketball players—United States—Biography—Juvenile literature.
Classification: LCC GV884.I88 (ebook) | LCC GV884.I88 L66 2019 (print) | DDC 796.323092 [B] —dc23

LC record available at https://lccn.loc.gov/2018060925

Manufactured in the United States of America
1-CG-7/15/19

CONTENTS

Kyrie Irving takes a shot while surrounded by Golden State Warriors players.

The arena was packed with cheering fans in a sea of golden jerseys. Kyrie Irving and his Cleveland Cavaliers were on the road against the Golden State Warriors. It was Game 7 of the 2016 National Basketball Association (NBA) Finals.

FACTS
AT A GLANCE

- **Date of Birth:** March 23, 1992

- **Position:** point guard

- **League:** NBA

- **Professional Highlights:** chosen by Cleveland Cavaliers as the first overall draft pick in 2011; named 2012 **Rookie** of the Year; traded to the Boston Celtics in 2017

- **Personal Highlights:** starred in the movie *Uncle Drew*; works with Best Buddies International to help people with special needs; visited Standing Rock **Reservation** to learn about his **heritage**

Irving dribbles past the Golden State Warriors' Festus Ezeli.

The **playoffs** against Golden State had been tough. At one point, the Cavaliers were down three games to one. They had to win the next three games in a row to earn the championship.

Cleveland took the next two games. But the Warriors were favorites. By Game 7, many thought Golden State would win. As the game neared its end, Irving raced down the court. He was being guarded by the Warriors' Stephen Curry. Irving took a shot and sunk a three-pointer. With ten seconds left in the game, the Cavaliers were leading 93–89. The Warriors ran back down the court but missed their shot. The buzzer rang out through the arena. Cleveland won!

Irving helped his team win its first NBA championship. And his final shot caught the attention of people across the NBA and beyond. "My life's changed drastically. . . . I never thought I'd be an NBA champion when I was 24 years old," Irving said.

Irving played with the Cavaliers for six years. He was then ready for a change. In 2017 the Cavaliers traded him to the Boston Celtics. It didn't take long for Irving to become a leader on his new team.

Irving hugs teammate LeBron James after the Cavaliers' championship in 2016.

GETTING TO THE NBA

In high school, Kyrie played on the 2010 McDonald's All-American boys team.

Kyrie Irving was born in Melbourne, Australia. His dad was a professional basketball player there. Both of Kyrie's parents were US citizens. So Kyrie had **dual citizenship** in Australia and the United States.

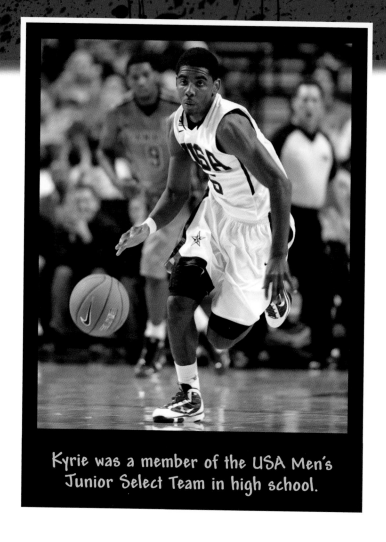
Kyrie was a member of the USA Men's Junior Select Team in high school.

Kyrie and his family moved to the United States when he was very young. Kyrie spent most of his childhood and teenage years in New Jersey. He played basketball in high school and was a leader on the team. He knew he wanted to play professionally, so he practiced a lot.

Kyrie was in his high school's production of *High School Musical*. He participated in the show to improve his public speaking skills.

Kyrie went on to play basketball at Duke University. Duke is a **powerhouse** program. During the 2010–2011 season, Kyrie played in only eleven games. He had to sit out for most of the season and the playoffs because of a toe injury. Still, people continued to notice his hard work.

In 2011, Kyrie entered the NBA Draft at 19 years old. The Cleveland Cavaliers chose him with the first pick of the draft. He signed with the Cavaliers and started as a point guard.

Kyrie played basketball at Duke University for a year.

Kyrie looks to pass the ball during a game in his rookie season.

People noticed his quick footwork and shooting ability. He developed into one of the NBA's best free throw shooters. The NBA named Kyrie the 2012 Rookie of the Year.

Kyrie's was one of the league's biggest stars when he was traded to the Celtics in 2017. He showed that he was a leader by helping his new teammates through difficult games and encouraging everyone to keep giving 100 percent.

PRACTICING AND HEALING

Irving takes a shot during practice.

A fan holds up a sign about Irving's knee injury.

Practice is very important to any athlete, including Irving. He spends hours exercising and practicing on the court every day. Still, even the best players get hurt. Injuries can keep players like Irving out of the game for months. When this happens, players heal through **rehabilitation.**

Irving practices shooting before the 2017 NBA Finals.

Irving has been injured several times during his basketball career. In April 2018 he had knee surgery and missed the playoffs with the Celtics. "It's a different off-season for me," he said when discussing the healing process. "It's a lot more time focusing on my body and getting mentally prepared for next season." Irving knows the importance of letting his body rest. When he gets back on the court, he needs to give everything he's got. When Irving plays basketball, he's quick on his feet. Players who guard him have a hard time guessing what he'll do next. But all of that footwork takes practice. Irving uses moves to get around defensive players.

Irving makes his way around Jimmy Butler during a Team USA practice.

Irving works to get around the Houston Rockets' James Harden.

These moves are not **spontaneous**. All of them are practiced. Irving practices dribbling the ball and spinning quickly on his feet. He wants his moves to surprise his opponents. Repeating these moves builds muscle memory that allows players to act fast without thinking. These quick actions could mean the difference between a win and a loss.

Point guards also need to have great ball-handling skills. Irving's coach helps him practice this. During practice, Irving dribbles a basketball. While he's dribbling, his coach throws more basketballs at him. Irving must catch the flying balls and throw them back while still dribbling the original ball. This takes a lot of strength and concentration.

Irving works hard to keep his skills sharp. But Irving also needs to stretch out his muscles. Stiff muscles can get injured more easily. Just as it's important for Irving to practice basketball, he also must keep his body healthy.

Irving gets ready to play defense during a 2017 game.

COMMUNITY CONNECTIONS

Irving gives his sneakers to a fan before a game in 2018.

Irving believes it's important to give back to the community. He knows that being an NBA player gives him the chance to do that. Irving works to help make other peoples' lives better.

Irving high-fives a girl participating in the Best Buddies program.

   Irving has been a part of Best Buddies International for years, even before he played in the NBA. Best Buddies International is a program that helps people with special needs. In 2016, Irving held a **benefit** for Best Buddies. The benefit included a one-mile (1.6-km) walk and a basketball game that Irving coached. The benefit raised thousands of dollars.

Irving has helped the community in other ways too. In 2018, he found out that his former high school in New Jersey needed a new gym. Irving helped pay for a new floor for the gym, plus a new locker room, weight room, and lounge.

Irving poses for a photo for the Best Buddies program.

Irving has also found ways to connect to his heritage. Irving and his older sister didn't know a lot about their mother because they were very young when she died. But Irving knew his mother was a member of the Standing Rock Lakota tribe. He mentioned this in an interview in 2016. **Elders** in the tribe saw the interview and found the names of Irving's grandparents.

Irving works with kids at basketball camps.

The elders invited Irving and his sister to participate in a naming ceremony to welcome them.

Irving speaks at Standing Rock
Indian Reservation.

At the Standing Rock Reservation in North Dakota, more than a thousand people gathered to watch the naming ceremony. Irving and his sister wore traditional Lakota clothing. Elders sang and prayed over them.

"Our journeys have been directed in so many different ways," Irving said. "But yet we are still standing here embracing each other as if we haven't lost any time."

From the NBA to the Movies

Irving has found many ways to connect with his community outside of basketball. In his 2016–2017 season with the Cavaliers, Irving starred in his first movie, *Uncle Drew*. The movie was filmed during the basketball season. It was a busy time. But Irving said that making movies and playing basketball weren't so different. Acting required a lot of repetition. He was used to that from practicing basketball.

Irving attends an event for his movie, *Uncle Drew*.

MOVING FORWARD

Irving brings the ball up the court while playing for the Celtics.

Irving started strong during his first year with the Celtics. But he had to cut his season short just before the playoffs. An infection had developed in his left knee.

Irving moves toward the basket during
a game against the Miami Heat.

Irving had to have surgery to get rid of the infection. It took him a long time to recover. Getting healthy required a lot of rest. Irving had to take medicine for two months and couldn't move his leg much. Then he went through **physical therapy** to strengthen his knee.

Irving handles the ball during a 2018 game.

By July 2018, Irving was able to start light practices again. He worked to be ready for the 2018–2019 season. The Celtics played the Cavaliers in November 2018. Irving led his team to a win by scoring 29 points. He proved that an injury couldn't keep him out of the game for long.

Irving doesn't know if he'll play with the Celtics forever. But he has said he loves playing basketball in Boston. "Obviously, a lot of great players have come before me, but to grow my name in Boston Celtics tradition and history is something I'm glad I can do," Irving said in October 2018.

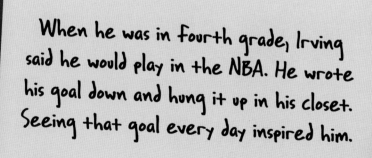

When he was in fourth grade, Irving said he would play in the NBA. He wrote his goal down and hung it up in his closet. Seeing that goal every day inspired him.

All-Star Stats

Kyrie Irving is one of the best free throw shooters in the NBA. He ranks among the top 10 active players in career shooting percentage for free throws.

Top 10 Free Throw Shooters Among Active Players as of 2018

1. Stephen Curry: 90%
2. JJ Redick: 89%
3. Damian Lillard: 88.5%
4. Kevin Durant: 88.2%
5. Kyle Korver: 88.1%
6. Dirk Nowitzki: 87. 94%
7. Isaiah Thomas: 87.6%
8. Kyrie Irving: 87.3%
9. Danilo Gallinari: 86.8%
10. Chris Paul: 86.7%

Source Notes

5. Joe Vardon, "Kyrie Irving: 'My Life's Changed Drastically' after Game 7 Shot," *Cleveland.com*, September 24, 2016, https://www.cleveland.com/cavs/index.ssf/2016/09/kyrie_irving_cavaliers.html

14. Sopan Deb, "Kyrie Irving Doesn't Know if the Earth Is Round or Flat. He Does Want to Discuss It," *New York Times*, June 8, 2018, https://www.nytimes.com/2018/06/08/movies/kyrie-irving-nba-celtics-earth.html

22. Brian Windhorst, "Kyrie Irving Goes through Naming Ceremony, Called Little Mountain," *ABC News*, August 23, 2018, https://abcnews.go.com/Sports/kyrie-irving-naming-ceremony-called-mountain/story?id=57360954

27. "Kyrie Irving Says He Became Sold on Celtics: 'I Believe in the Franchise,'" *ESPN*, October 6, 2018, http://www.espn.com/nba/story/_/id/24905161/kyrie-irving-staying-boston-celtics-happy-here

Glossary

benefit: an event held to raise money for an organization or cause

dual citizenship: official status as a citizen in more than one country

elders: older people, especially those who are respected or have authority

heritage: history and traditions passed down through the generations in a group of people

physical therapy: the treatment of diseased or injured muscles and joints using techniques such as exercise, massage, and heat

playoffs: games after the regular season that determine which teams will compete for the championship

powerhouse: strong

rehabilitation: the process of healing an injury

reservation: an area of land set aside by the government for Native Indian tribes to live on

rookie: an athlete who is in his first season with a professional sports team

spontaneous: random or sudden without thinking

Further Information

Fishman, Jon M. *Kyrie Irving*. Minneapolis: Lerner
  Publications, 2017.

Goodman, Michael E. *Boston Celtics*. Mankato, MN: Creative
  Education, 2018.

Kyrie Irving Best Buddies Page
https://www.bestbuddies.org/tag/kyrie-irving/

Kyrie Irving Boston Celtics Bio
https://www.nba.com/celtics/roster/profiles?pid=202681

Kyrie Irving Career Stats
https://www.basketball-reference.com/players/i/irvinky01.html

Index

Photo Acknowledgments

The images in this book are used with permission of: © Bob Donnan/Getty Images Sport/Getty Images, pp. 4–5; © Marcio Jose Sanchez/AP Images, p. 6; © Eric Risberg/AP Images, p. 7; © Jim Rinaldi/Icon SMI/Icon Sport Media/Icon Sportswire/Getty Images, p. 8; © Chris Ryan/Corbis/Corbis Sport/Getty Images, p. 9; © Lance King/Icon SMI/Icon Sport Media/Icon Sportswire/Getty Images, p. 10; © David Dermer/Diamond Images/Getty Images, p. 11; © Gregory Shamus/Getty Images Sport/Getty Images, p. 12; © Adam Glanzman/Getty Images Sport/Getty Images, p. 13; © Ezra Shaw/Getty Images Sport/Getty Images, p. 14; © Ethan Miller/Getty Images Sport/Getty Images, p. 15; © Tim Warner/Getty Images Sport/Getty Images, p. 16; © Omar Rawlings/Getty Images Sport/Getty Images, pp. 17, 18; © Stephen Lovekin/Getty Images Entertainment/Best Buddies/Getty Images, pp. 19, 20; © Denise Truscello/WireImage/Getty Images, p. 21; © Mike McCleary/The Bismarck Tribune/AP Images, p. 22; © lev radin/Shutterstock.com, p. 23; © Bob Levey/Getty Images Sport/Getty Images, p. 24; © Michael Reaves/Getty Images Sport/Getty Images, p. 25; © Christian Petersen/Getty Images Sport/Getty Images, p. 26.

Front Cover: © Adam Glanzman/Getty Images Sport/Getty Images.